i am so tired of feeling this way.
By Rhys Harding

Illustrations by Kay Wilson

Introduction

Moving within spaces where you can breathe and others where you cannot. Hiding from the world and exposing yourself as a fraud. Taking on too much and eating too little. Struggling to find the right moments to speak. Finding yourself messing up time and time again. Welcome to *i am so tired of feeling this way*.

How do we as people navigate our world with ease and sanity? This collection tries to discover our deepest anxieties and cope with extreme bounds of love lost. Through starvation, degradation, placing yourself in danger, and questioning even feeling alive: these are all natural human responses, yet still we find them hard to discuss.

Whenever you feel yourself ooze and tip over with rage, know that these words already exist in the book you're reading. Whenever you feel heartbroken, lost, and confused, there are words in here which try to encapsulate the feeling on these pages. Read them, breathe them in, and let them rise from your chest into thin air. There will always be moments in time where we are all tired of feeling.

Spanning from late 2015 to the present day, this collection has lived a life which has been a struggle, both mentally and physically. There is no real agenda here other than it wanting to exist. As the collection becomes physical and in digital formats, for all to digest, *i am so tired of feeling this way.* asks you to leave your notions behind. It's important to allow yourself to feel. If you're going to read poetry – it's a given you already know the rules – but we need to be clear: this is a time for reflection and perhaps even enjoyment.

There will be moments in time where the world feels as if it is crumbling around you. Moments where the discussion of these topics mentioned in this book will be difficult to say aloud to your loved ones. Move with the wind and the grass blows you forward. Do not look back at the times you cannot fix or control. When we pile up the boxes, things feel heavier. We see less because they're piled on top of one another. This collection wants you to let go of all of that. Find your own way of breaking down this barrier that sits around you. Give yourself the space to think and feel. Picture yourself in your favourite setting and let your mind run wild. When we feel it, we can feel ourselves transform to something new.

This is ultimately a glorified journal, one with words and pictures that heavily relate to one another. It's personal with the aim of wanting to be universal. It is as much a story as it is an autobiography. It now belongs to you.

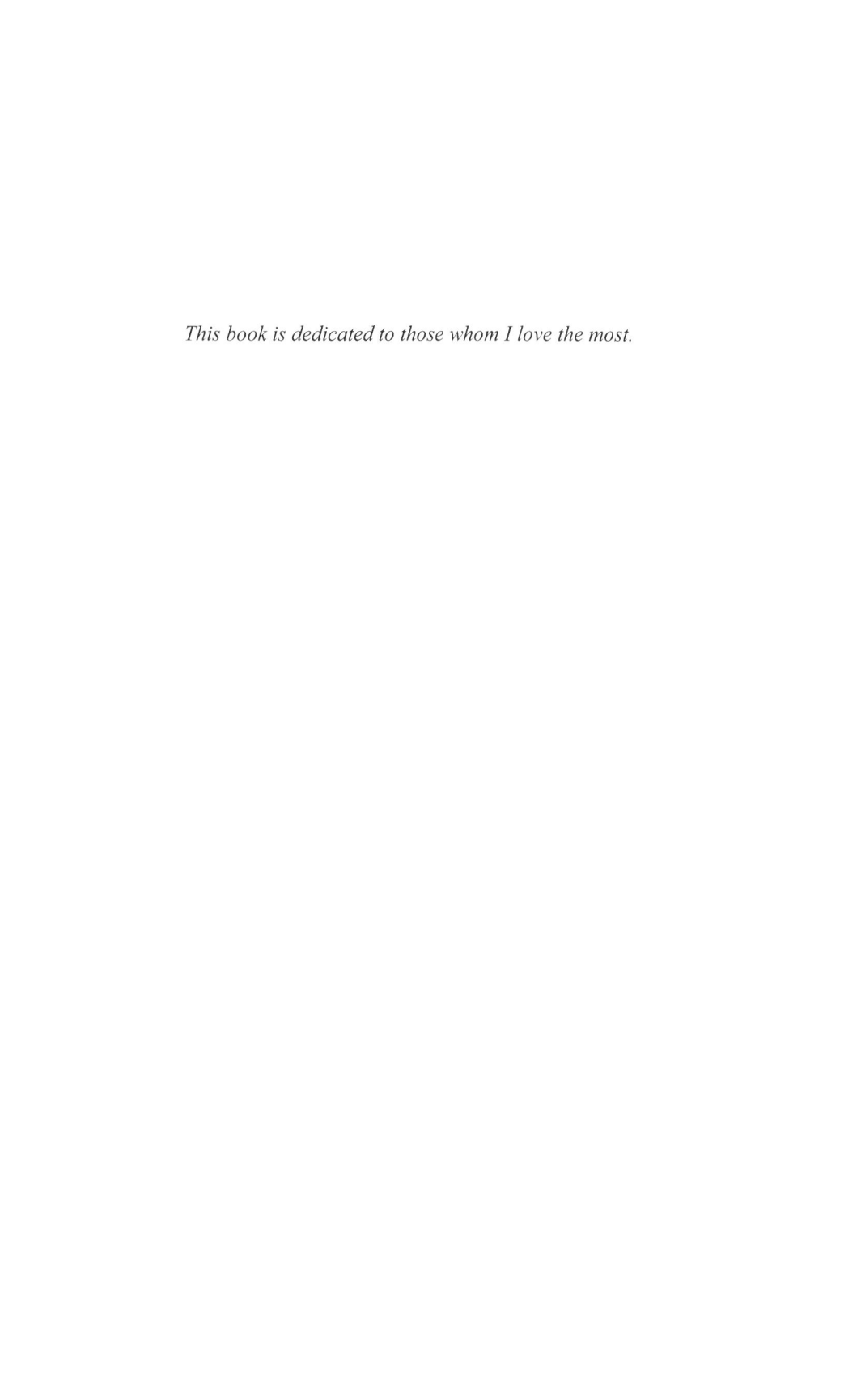

This book is dedicated to those whom I love the most.

his
skin no longer smells of water
but i
am drowning
and he
is walking
i am
sinking
and he
is breathing
my lungs are collapsing
tulips on his flesh
now i
am brooding
and he
is serene
gone in 5 minutes
i am
quiet
he is
loud.

                                                                          he -

the aisle
exists
just as much
as i walk down it.
underlying
are pills
that i hid
inside the pews
ready to take
when i felt ready.
a catharsis
that only exists
if you believe
the grass can speak
the stone can hear
the sky can see
and the altar can taste
your anxiety.
petals fall one by one
i am ready
to catch them
and lick
their scent.

departing from my current self –

dialogue
builds a fortress
in my ribcage
it crowns
my heart
like the weight
of scrambled eggs
on our plate
this saturday.
you removed your power to touch
yet here you are in the wind
still
clawing
every
surface
of
my
skin.

                                              cruel love –

it seems that my trauma sticks
to my skin wherever i go.

feel the warmth on your lips
as you shower at midnight.
delegating your emotions from afar
is easy when you're willing to hide
in a tight space where no one can find you.

                                                    stop blaming yourself -

it will get
stormy through my
mouth which encompass
the thigh of my
lover and the
blood on
walls of yellow
that drink from
the voices
of people you have never
had contact with
touch you in
your most vulnerable.
grown up
aware of the stains
you finally scrub
your coat.

8 sessions of counselling —

                                              you show
                                                   me
                              sleet on your pinky finger
                                             you feed
                                                   me
                             the turquoise sitting down
                                          it breathes
                              and it falls from the sky
                                           a stranger
                     turns the light on with its beak
                                         we exchange
                                              glances
                                        time to get up
                                          and jump.

                                   6 months of anxiety –

Crave

All I need is for you to crave me. So, I can feel as if being needed was always the right thing to feel. A satisfaction so pure and sacred that I know for a fact that it can't be true. I am teething a love so bitter when I swallow, I can feel the teeny, tiny blades cut the inside of my throat. Feeling the scratch in my throat, I grab my throat and squeeze. Crave. Me. Choking by the kitchen cabinet, I am alone and yet being watched by every ghost on this street, begging me not to join them because I haven't finished my purpose yet. I have no purpose, maybe I would if I could sense you lusting after me. I feel nervous in a way I haven't felt before. I dreamt of being inside a house similar to this, but not this house.

do they
touch you
like
i can
like the yoghurt
drips down
the skirting boards
i'd trace my hands
under your
bottom lashes
and whisper
knowing
i can scream
i can not
touch you
not anymore
and in this sharp autumn
i am surviving
without your palm.

touch -

i wish you fucked somebody else because at least i wouldn't have your spirit lingering in my bedroom.

the room that won't leave -

come inside
and explore
my hollow skin
set it on fire
then leave.
my healing is sacred
i am unaware of
what fixes me
but
i know what shatters me.
the shy poltergeist
i pick you up
feed your throat with thread
pulling out the implausible
but one word clings
to my kneecap.

heal –

Your gaze sharpens my soul
And I can't help but miss
The feeling of you hating me.

Mercury drips down my chest
The curvature around my nipple, it hardens.
I swallow my phlegm like sawdust
Hoping tomorrow will be more successful.

The night is always described as mysterious
Sometimes eerie.
It's calming.
Because I can hear the wind breathe against my palms
The back of my knees
I only shiver because the dead are trying to communicate.
Maybe if we stayed outside
A little longer
A little later
We would hear their thoughts a little louder.

I feel nauseous
When I remember
You probably don't think of me
Deep down in the ocean
The thoughts you buried deep.
Tie to my bed
Notes from the ghosts of the people you once were
Whispering **i love you**
I want you to kiss every inch of my body
Not caring of my imperfections
That I see every morning after I step out of the shower
I am here and waiting
Crying tonight because I know you're no longer coming.

The night –

hurting is here
and it will not leave my home.
it strokes my chest
and decides for me
the torture of the day.
the room blackens
and the hurt will linger on my back
for i am the only one who can lift it
and throw it away.
but i am weak
and the burden prolongs.
piece by piece
i will tear it down
the hurt begins to vomit
it vomits on my earlobe
and i hear it paint my nostril
hurt used to surrender
but tonight it thrives
it squeezes and pushes
and i begin to lie
in this hospital bed
why did they let me go when hurt still sits on my chest?

hurt -

Roots

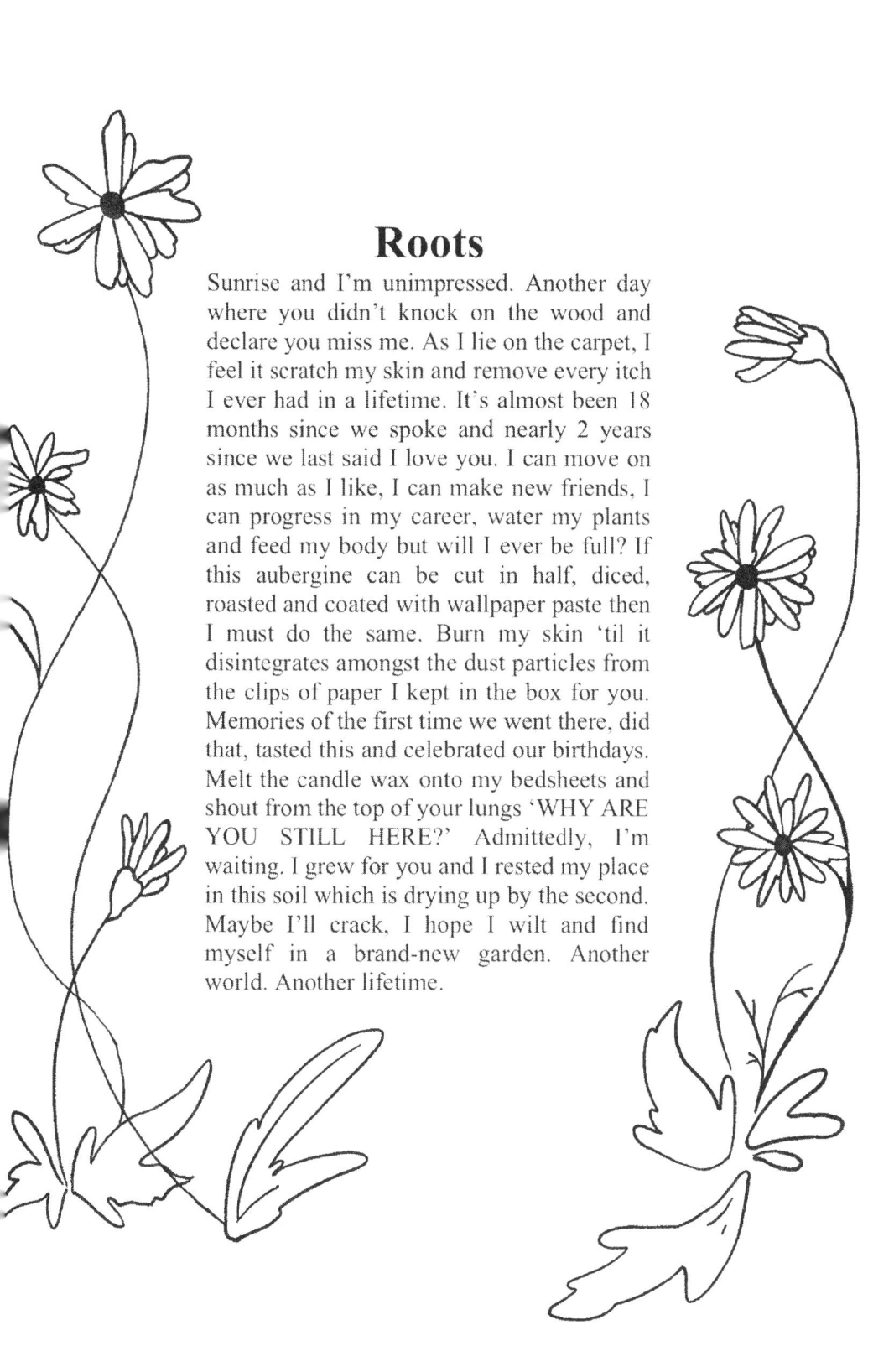

Sunrise and I'm unimpressed. Another day where you didn't knock on the wood and declare you miss me. As I lie on the carpet, I feel it scratch my skin and remove every itch I ever had in a lifetime. It's almost been 18 months since we spoke and nearly 2 years since we last said I love you. I can move on as much as I like, I can make new friends, I can progress in my career, water my plants and feed my body but will I ever be full? If this aubergine can be cut in half, diced, roasted and coated with wallpaper paste then I must do the same. Burn my skin 'til it disintegrates amongst the dust particles from the clips of paper I kept in the box for you. Memories of the first time we went there, did that, tasted this and celebrated our birthdays. Melt the candle wax onto my bedsheets and shout from the top of your lungs 'WHY ARE YOU STILL HERE?' Admittedly, I'm waiting. I grew for you and I rested my place in this soil which is drying up by the second. Maybe I'll crack, I hope I wilt and find myself in a brand-new garden. Another world. Another lifetime.

dying of daydreams
i lie and i contemplate
if the glitter on my thigh
would disappear like you did.
through the draft of my window
the bitterness covers me and
i am wearing my favourite sadness
and the picture you drew me
sits in the box down the hallway.
as much as i try
to ignore
the ink
will still bleed
on this paper
and the glitter
will sit
in the plant pots
on my desk
and bury
in the fibres
of my rug.
pink
is a striking colour.

glitter –

so you shave your head and take your pills and convince yourself no one has ever felt the way you are feeling right now.

5 weeks after –

i need
the clouds to dress me
i need to be okay
just for tonight
because tomorrow
i can begin to get stronger
i can place the sorrow in my drawer
i need
to walk these fields
alone
i'll tell you 'i miss you'
i'll hope for your return
but i won't expect your soul
to be the same or to be there at all.

                                        travelling is therapeutic –

Falling in and out of love feels like a cruel privilege.
                        We don't deserve it
              but we all share it,   caress it,
lose it,   find it again,
                        scratched by it and we sit staring at
our belly buttons,   wondering what goes
on inside and out.   Now you're gone
and I am fully over you, I am still confused.   drink
this eat that smell this and tell me it's not love, because it's all I'm
sensing.   Grinding my teeth,   like
I'm struggling to get these words to
             form some shape with my lips.   I am
still casting spells   grasping the leaves that drip from the
tap and hoping they will bleed just like I do.

                                            Untitled 14/04/2019 -

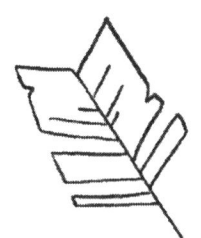

Trying not to love you

It's wild to see myself fall in love with you. I thought the word love was more sacred than this. Like in those romantic books or poetry anthologies. Love is ethereal, almost unnatural, yet completely real. Sitting beside you makes my stomach somersault. Makes my stomach cry in pain. It shouts and I cover its mouth with my hands. Makes my stomach feel so eerie it's no longer describable. Makes my stomach feel so, so fragile but strong enough to handle you punching me right in my gut. Watching you get up and leave for five minutes is excruciating. I wish a doctor would come and spoon out my organs like a nearly finished pot of jam. Lick their fingers and say, I did it, love no longer exists. Honestly, that would be the perfect situation. When you come back it's like Diane Keaton got back home and confessed her love that never went away for her husband. I'd like that. A romcom moment. My own. Does that mean it's more real? Probably the opposite, but who's judging? Just myself. Right now, that's the only thing that matters.

i donate my love to you
because tonight you need it
and tomorrow I won't want it
so i'll pass it back to you.

sit down and place your head
against the cold stone that holds up your home
think of the times we spent together
when i poured you water
and you thanked me for it.

looking back into the blueness of it all
i understood how you loved me
but i could never see it before
for that i am sorry.
i don't want or need your forgiveness
but i continue to donate my love
as a symbol that my love is real
even when i'm purposely making it seem like it isn't.

i donate my love to you
i can feed you my love
i can nourish your stomach 'til it stops bleeding all the love i gave you
until we say goodbye on this bed of grass
that marks my trousers and makes me aware i'm dirty
with water trickling down my face
and blood creeping through the cracks of the ceiling
i understand it now
i get what you were trying to show me
and for that i leave you with my love forever.

                                            I donate my love to you -

your heart opens
the sigh from the daisies
lingers like the hangnail on your index finger
you ask yourself, how much do i love myself today?

sitting down requires more effort than before
because you bruised your back in the bathtub.
read another chapter of your book
drink some juice and stroke your skin
tomorrow might be the same.

take out your problems one by one
place them on the table
line them up, divide them in two
then mix them up again and throw them in the bin
right now all you need to do is breathe
you watch some television show
you might revisit that one again tomorrow.

untitled 29/05/2020 -

i feel correct for five minutes
because i was granted permission
to feed myself with affection.

it was sweet
the way you could say hello
and leave again
without crows squawking in my stomach.

i want to go home tonight
light a candle
pray to something or another
soak my skin and run my hands on every nook
catching splinters and tasting the wood.

tonight i ate and we are celebrating that.

                      I haven't had a real meal in 5.25 days –

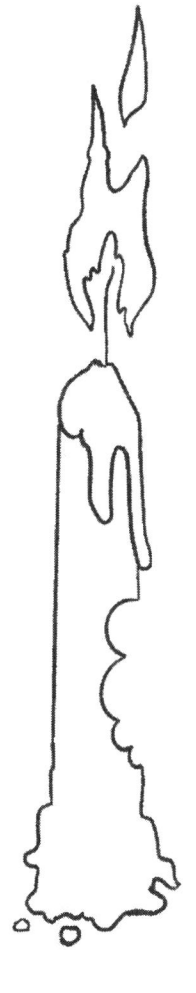

Piano

Anybody can play the piano if they place their fingers on one. Any person can jump out of a moving vehicle if they have the courage. I haven't left my bed all weekend because I was concerned if I did, I'd fall back into my terrible habits. Lie still, lie back, lie down. Lie to the side, lie on your stomach just like a slice of cucumber that sits on the ceramic plate you bought five years ago. This was when you began your life. When you thought you had it all figured out and the contingency plan was working out perfectly.

It was windy by the sea, but it didn't matter because you thought you had moved on. You were sorting it out piece by piece but that weekend somebody ran away with the rest of the box. Turns out you picked up the wrong game anyway. Maybe I should start to play the piano now.

Listen to the voices in your head and decipher which one is your best friend. You'll always make the wrong choice because it's never meant to go perfectly the first time. Or second. Or the third. I am on my fourth go, I think. I don't know. I've lost count but at least I know how to play a few chords on the piano.

Regurgitating all the broken sentences I swallowed when you were here.

Should've told you everything I felt even if it meant I'd make a fool of myself.

My teeth feel like mini plastic forks, all congregated together inside my mouth for a stabbing directly on my tongue. How dare you sit there in silence? Sit and say nothing.

I still have a pair of your socks and I never want to give them back. You have a pair of mine too. I hope you never throw them away.

Something about the way I miss you being upset with me. Something about the way I said nothing and I quite liked it. Something about the way we kissed for hours and never got tired. Something about the way we would roll on each other and stroke each other's hair, listen to our favourite music and let the hours pass us by. Maybe that was a waste of time in hindsight but it was the only way we could be together. *The only time we knew how to be together.*

Nothing can come close to the moments I'd wrap my thighs around your waist and hug you... like you've just given birth to me and now I'm here in this world with you. Leave our clothes on the floor and cinch my waist so tight I can feel your hands inside my stomach. That's when I'll know you really love me.

   Regurgitating all the broken sentences I swallowed -

was our love limited to this space
because i am in Berlin
and i don't feel love from you.

i'm in Painshill
and these rocks whispered
everything was okay
when it was not,

we sit on this coach
you loved me on the motorway
you loved me in London.

i kiss your neck in Edinburgh
and we didn't know
that was the highest we would go
and this was just our love beginning.

                                                         love in different places -

seeing you again was like biting cloth.
pull it with your teeth
hide it here
and hide it there.
pull it apart
so strangers can wince
friends can feel unsettled
mum can tell you again how worried she is
because she heard it as well.

you can't swallow cloth
you can try but it hurts
and you'll probably spew it back up anyway
i know that for fact.
i am completely silent for the first time
so why can't you hear me now?
TWO YEARS

it's been two years
i tried to not look at you
and i did it so well

pull me aside
tear the cloth that sits
that is buried
burning inside your body
use your nails to claw it out
i'm begging now, speak.

the inheritance -

i was told
to look after you
fingertips which smoke my hearing
i was informed you would be fine
the ocean dresses you soaked with weights
you are pale blue
you are turning inside out
your organs dress you now
your skin is no longer dense
riotous
you surrender
admit your oblivions
suffer your integrity
move with the grass
allow the rain
to digest your insecurities
run slow you are still young.

talking to my body –

Soothing

Feeling the warmth on your face from the sun is soothing. It hugs you like your favourite food. It digests like the embrace of your most loved friend. And as I sit in the car waiting for my mum to return, I remember the days I felt truly happy.

falling asleep is difficult
whilst you're awake
because i want to hold your hand
every waking second

right under my toes
lies the grass and i question
why the only thing i can feel
is your head that you're pressing against mine?

my soul feels soft and weak today
because you smile at me like you loved me
and i felt my knees wobble around
like a kid out of control.

i must remember to breathe
and talk to myself to acknowledge this feeling is real
i've always wanted to feel this way
yet as it happens
i am completely frightened.

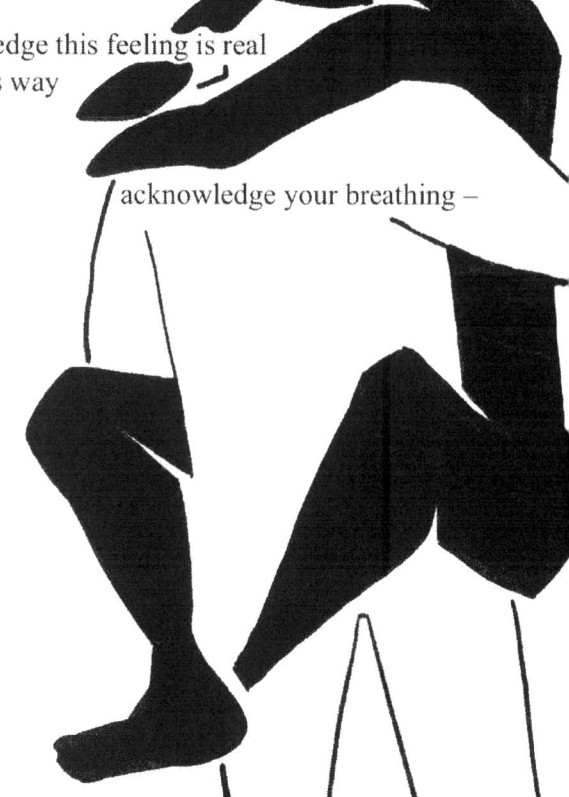

acknowledge your breathing –

what if we played video games together?
would you like it?
times have really changed
and i'm slightly confused
to be feeling warm inside my belly.

i worship the cobbles
your feet walk on.
i wish i could tell you
that i quite like the way you yawned
and smiled after like you were pleased
even though i know
you smiled because i was staring.

i enjoy watching you live
and i'm so jealous
to see you walk without an inch of anxiety.
if you let me touch your hair
i don't think i'd let go.

                                                            i'm here in Italy –

chew me up
and say it with musk
so i can smell your words
and sing from my eyes
with grace
i embarrass the dead grass
for not even bothering to listen
to the wants and needs
of my surroundings.

                                      punishment is starting with the garden –

can it wait
a little longer
while i take this space to breathe
and think of a moment
when it felt salty to grab
the drainpipe
holding myself up
thinking of a way to escape
without anyone noticing.

i see
the ocean as
a means of survival
biting the inside
of my cheeks
look to the sky
and embody
the whole world tonight.

i really miss you and i can't tell you that –

have you ever had a word stick to the roof of your mouth? i'm trying to scratch it off with my tongue to see if what i had to say was even worthwhile.

                                              is it time to go back into therapy? –

i consume the brown leaves
and remember your dad's old jumper you used to lend me.

if we met again, i would want you to know that i'm doing better
that i still drink coffee and imagine waking up next to you
sniffing the bedsheets that smell half fresh and the other half, your
skin.

if i got to touch you again i would be so quiet so you wouldn't flinch
and tell me it was bad to feel you again i would press my finger
against my own lips and hope to recreate that one moment we had
before where you would grab my body and claim it as your own.

i seek your forgiveness not to atone my sins but for the knowing that
you still see me because my god, i see you with my cold breath in the
winter and when the sun flashes in my eyes through the cracks of the
leaves in trees.

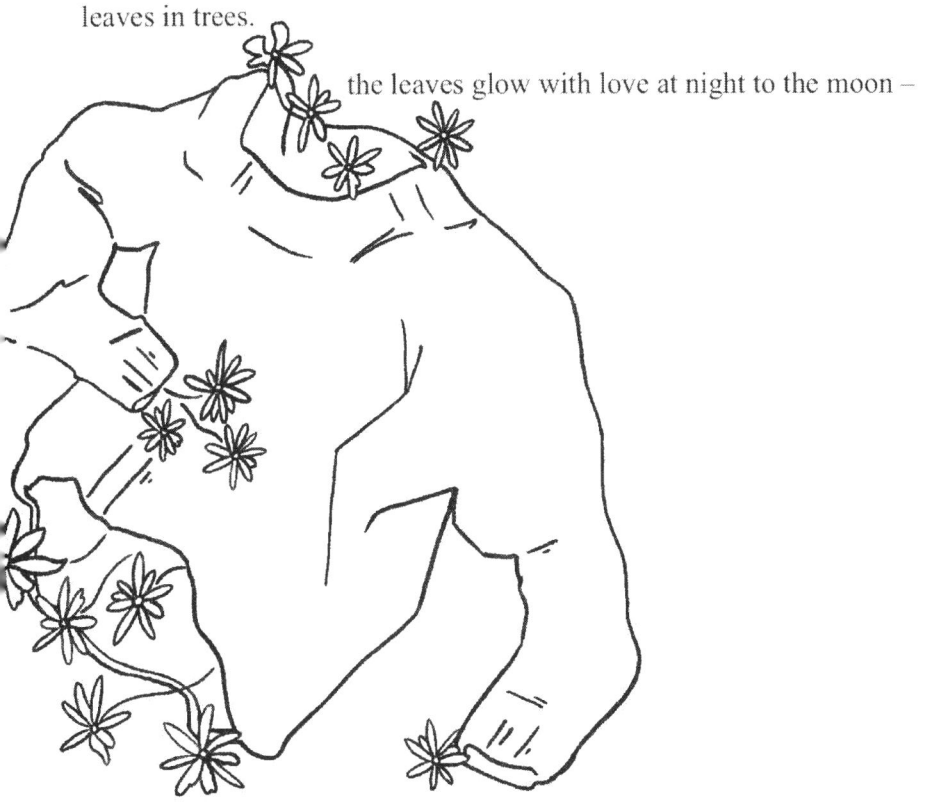

the leaves glow with love at night to the moon –

Printed in Great Britain
by Amazon